Published by Pop-O Books 2018

www.popobooks.com.au

Copyright © 2018 Tanya Popovski

Illustrations by Chris McQuinlan

http://chrismacquinlanart.artstation.com

Copying of this book for educational purposes: All rights reserved. No part of this publication may be reproduced, stored in a retrieval system, or transmitted in any form or by any means, electronic, mechanical, photocopying, recording or otherwise, without the prior written permission from the publisher.

A catalogue record for this book is available from the National Library of Australia.

Book cover design and formatting services by BookCoverCafe.com

First edition 2018

ISBN 978-0-6484160-1-2

Acknowledgements

Thank you to my family David, Kirsten and Jacob. To my parents Anthony and Rosy Mintoff, and my sisters Sylvia, Michelle and Chantelle for being my cheerleaders and always supporting me. I am very lucky to have grown up in such a wonderful family with great memories of our childhood. Now looking forward to growing old in your company.

Hello, my name is Harry and I'm sure we have met before. You probably know me as a common housefly, but my scientific name is *Musca domestica*.

I love to fly around your home, and sometimes when I find a mirror I stop to have a good look at myself.

I love my wings. I have two sets. The main pair helps me to fly, and the smaller pair keeps me balanced so I don't wobble when I'm buzzing through the air.

My tongue is shaped like a straw, and I use it to slurp up my food.

And just look at my beautiful eyes. Did you know that flies' eyes are the most complicated in the insect world?

They're called compound eyes, which means they're made up of many repeating units called ommatidia. Having ommatidia means I can detect the smallest of movements that other creatures may miss. I use my feet to rub my eyes clean because I don't have eyelids like you do.

As I buzz around, landing on anything and everything, I can carry up to 33 million diseases from plants, animals or bacteria. This means that you need to be careful when I'm around. It's especially important that you are hygienic and wash your hands before you eat. You might not have seen me, but I could have landed on your desk, pen or bag when you weren't looking.

It's not all bad; I can help the police solve murders. People who study insects like me are called entomologists. These scientists are able to tell when a death has taken place just by looking at insects at the scene. My friends and I are proud to be an important part of that process.

Flies are also very useful to doctors. Baby flies, also known as maggots, can be used to help people who have injuries to their flesh. These clever maggots eat the damaged flesh and this helps the wound to heal.

For example, doctors might use the help of baby flies with someone who has been badly burnt.

I once heard that you think flies are pests. How could you think that, after all we do? We help the environment by breaking down food waste and it only takes us a couple of days. We pollinate flowers, control other pests, and provide food for birds and fish. Would a pest do all those good things?

Doing all this work has made me quite tired. I think I'll go and sit in my favourite spot out of the wind.

So the next time you see me buzzing around and want to swat me, stop for a moment and think about all the good that flies do.

About the Author

Tanya Popovski has a Bachelor of Education from the University of Wollongong, and over twenty-five years of teaching experience working with primary school-aged children. She is also a mother of two children. Tanya's experience moves beyond the classroom and into the realms of special education, behaviour support, literacy support, NAPLAN analysis, and development and training in the area of Focus on Reading.

Tanya's passion is educating children to be the best that they can be. She understands the key role that parents play in their child's education as the first educators in their child's life. Giving parents access to explicit teaching and good questioning can only have a positive impact on their child's learning, by being exposed daily to the process of analysing, synthesising and evaluating texts. With these skills, children will be better equipped to apply these thinking skills to any text within a subject area.

PoP-O Books offers a way to explicitly teach important comprehension skills through discussion. Annotated questions and answers help to target questions found in NAPLAN.

Learn with

Amelia Faces Her Anxiety
(picture book + question guide)

Everyone feels some level of anxiety at different times and Amelia is no different.
She wants to go on year 5's overnight trip, but she's very worried about it. What will she do? Will she face her anxiety or give in?

Sebastian's Monster
(picture book + question guide)

Sebastian is too scared to go to sleep at night because he knows there's a monster in his room. Any child would expect their parents to tell them they're imagining things and there are no such

things as monsters. Instead, Sebastian's mum begins to ask many strange questions about the monster he has seen in his room.
What is going on?

Cranky Corey
(picture book + question guide)

Everyone knows someone like Corey. When things don't go to plan during sporting games, he always throws tantrums and storms off the field.
Will Corey's friends tell him the truth about his behaviour?
Will he accept responsibility for his tantrums?

New Title Coming Soon

The Pretend Friend
(picture book + question guide)

Mikayla and Bella have always been the best of friends. They are like two peas in a pod and their parents joke that they're joined at the hip.
But things change when they reach high school, and the two best friends begin to drift apart. Mikayla feels like she's being left out. After she starts being bullied on social media, she realises that Bella isn't supportive the way she used to be. Perhaps Bella was never a true friend at all.

Each title includes:

- Reader's storybook
- Annotated storybook with questions and answers
- Tracking sheet linked to the Australian curriculum (sold separately at www.popobooks.com.au)

Mid–Upper Primary

Running Words 451
Text Type: Narrative

www.ingramcontent.com/pod-product-compliance
Lightning Source LLC
Chambersburg PA
CBHW062107290426
44110CB00022B/2739